Now is a Moveable Feast

BY THE AUTHOR

LONG TONGUE
RETURN SINGLE

NOW IS A
MOVEABLE FEAST

A POEM AND DRAWINGS

by Anne Le Marquand Hartigan

ISBN 0 948339 54 3   Hardcover

ISBN 0 948339 55 1   Softcover

Salmon Publishing

Bridge Mills

Galway

Cover and illustrations by Anne Hartigan

Typeset by Phototype-Set Ltd. and Designed by

Raymond Kyne Design Associates, Dublin

Printed by Colour Books, Dublin

Hardback Binding by Kenny's Fine Binding, Galway

DEDICATION

For my mother, Elizabeth,
her mother, Gertrude,

for Dominic Mark Herome Marianne Elizabeth Hugh,
Kirsty Alison Sophie Brendan Tim Mary,
Diarmuid Florence Colm Elizabeth Inis Patrick Zöe Cherri Naoise and Terry.

ACKNOWLEDGMENTS

Radio Telefís Eireann broadcast *Now is a Moveable Feast* with music composed by Eibhlis Farrell. Sections of this poem appeared in *Salmon Magazine* and *The Dundalk Magazine*, and were sung as *'Songs of Death'*, with music by Eibhlis Farrell, at the Hugh Lane Gallery, Dublin.

INTRODUCTION

An introduction is, I suppose, a signpost, or a trail of breadcrumbs to the magic part of the forest. I had two ambitions when I embarked on what became *Now is a Moveable Feast*: to write a poem about a house — the house my mother was born in, and to write a long work.

The voices in the poem are those who lived there in the past, now, and in a possible future. Among the human voices there is my grandfather, a real patriach, with whom my grandmother had a 'made marriage'. She died from pernicious anemia after separation from her husband; as my mother put it, she was 'taken away' by her parents. Then my grandmother's sister Lily, who died along with her infant in childbirth because her husband refused to let her go to Dublin for medical attention. My great-grandmother is there, à strong women. It is a poem that celebrates women, but, over and through, under and in everything is the ever-enduring land. The land links us with prehistory, history and myth; with the sea, sky, birds, animals and the continuous flow of the great River Boyne itself.

When the poem was completed in 1979, Professor Brendan Kennelly suggested that I send it to RTE. Dick Warner did a production of it for radio in 1980. It was a joy to work with him and the enthusiastic cast. Through this I made friends with Eibhlis Farrell, who composed the music for that production. She also wrote a beautiful song cycle (Songs of Death) for sections of the poem, and these were performed at the Hugh Lane Gallery in Dublin. My warm thanks to them. Since then, I have given readings around Ireland and in New York with Cathy Leeney, Moria Mulcahy, Biba and Hugh Hartigan. Among our venues were the Dublin Lit Fest, at the Dublin Millennium celebrations, the International Yeats Summer School in Sligo and Listowel Writers' Week. It was so enjoyable to work with them, and I give them my grateful thanks.

Anne Le Marquand Hartigan

Dublin, January 1991

C ONTENTS

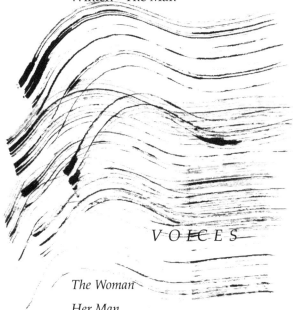

VOICES

TOWNLAND

God: 'One generation passeth away,

and another generation cometh:

but the earth standeth for ever.'

ECCLESIASTES 1.4

Auctioneer: This desirable old-world residence is in a highly

sought-after area. Standing in its own grounds,

it is in a commanding position overlooking

river and sea . . . .

This house
peers
out
through trees.

Slowly
as the year
turns,

she unpeels
a white
face.

12

Browns

recede,

then branches

trace

thin

tightropes

through the air.

A house laid bare.

    Desire

    Desire

The jackdaws call

And clear cluck

On the evening air

A bat of wings

In the beeches' hair

Dart down and weave

A skein of black

The cluckling chorus

Sing tick tack

To nest in the chimney's eyes
Brick-a-brack,

They tig tag
And chuck their humour

At the skies
Back.

Auctioneer: This desirable old-world residence standing in
               its own grounds is in a commanding position,
               with views of river and sea, surrounded by
               mature trees . . . .

The position was . . . commanding.
The position was . . . detached.

Stand
to command,
the bend
of the land
to his hand,

the tith
and tilt
of soil,
oil to his back;

hard held
against
any loss or lack
George or Jack,

against invader.

> Can I hear the Viking cry
> On the water, water,
> Who is slipping up the river?

> Daughter
> Daughter.

Hard hand
held the reins
tight.

Sent horses
back.
The brasses

must bright
lighten the world.

Gleam
my diamonds
my pearls.

The position:

In the beginning
was a man.
Who was a hard man,

and wild with it
he was seen,
(God love us)

shoot clean
and neat
as ever,

a little cockerel
cowering,
between a small child's feet.

I can hear the redshank call

His voice in sharp warning

Who is slipping up the tide

This dim morning?

The position:

Was commanding.

Was desirable.

Was surrounded by mature trees.

We had a commanding position
said the rook,

I was told
by those aged and old
how our ancestors left
this high landing.

No nesting
no nook
was safe.

Our brotherhood forsook
this promised land,
driven and riven

as pistol point
blast and shook
our skyholds,

our rafts
scattered
on the sea's breeze.

Black feathers
died red,
on our crown
of thorns.

We do not remember
the gradual returning
when we returned to

this former position,
we are not bothered

as we tidy and tighten
our nests in the springtime

our droppings whiten
the green of the garden,

our eyes overlook
our wings command

river and shore
river and land

the position commands.

Auctioneer: This desirable family residence stands detached
                      and secluded on two hundred acres of prime
                      farm land . . . .

God: 'One generation passeth away,
              and another generation cometh:'

              The position:

              Was desirable,
              Was detached,
              Was two hundred acres,

              There was no desire.

Where will the white tern go?
Where can she dip or fly?
Daughter you must go
Down where the curlews cry.

Come daughter come,
By the Boyne river stand
Come daughter sweet daughter
You will take his hand,

Sweet daughter dear daughter
You must understand,
We have found you a husband
Who is well blessed with land.

Where will the white tern go?
Where dip where start?
Where will she flash her wings?
Her dive to the heart,
Where waters slash apart.

LAND

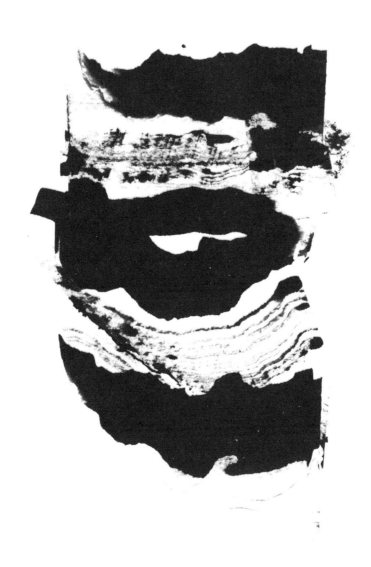

Auctioneer: This desirable family residence of old-world
                     charm detached and secluded on prime farm
                     land. The entire property is for sale by private
                     treaty.

They were bound
    by Church and State,
man and mate.

                     No impediment was found;

no consanguinity,
    affinity,
no spiritual relationship.

The contract was signed,
    was sealed,
underlined and delivered.

                     'And thou shalt be under thy husband's power.'

They were tied
    man and maid,
were wedded

married and bedded,
  delivered?
The land, must prove,

must know, must pass,
  from hand to hand,
from Father to Son,

      the need, in the cut of the plough,

the yearn
  for seed,
the ache
  for increase

to cleave
  penetrate
and grow,

      'And he shall have dominion over thee.'

The contract was signed,
  was sealed,
was delivered.

Now under his power
  under his dominion,
the lamb

to the altar
   a dumb hurt,
the double crunch

   of Church
   on duty.

Out of that dominion
growing,
a list,
towards love,

a twist in the meaning,
in that stony season.

Day and night ruled,
and reasoned, out.

'Blessed are the poor
for they shall have their fill.

Blessed are the sorrowful
for they shall be comforted,

Blessed are the meek,
for they shall possess the land.'

MATTHEW 5. 3-5

This new clay
was cut,
the first of the year.

The sharp edge.
The steel hiss
a pledge,

the plough's
first kiss.
Turning

young soil
to heaven.
Now on her back,

veiled white
with the hack
of hoar frost,

the cold
fingers and fumbles
this brown dress,

crumbles you
with his caress
under his icy eye

weeds wither
and die;
on your harrowed bed

you lie
quick with need,
seed

scattered
and spread,
wide open

to a vast sky.

Mother when you bade me
Take his hand to dance.

Do the will of God dear
this is the only chance.

I obeyed you Mother
without a second glance
took me to my duties
learnt to do the dance.

It is the will of God dear,
nothing's left to chance.

Her mountain was not more difficult
Than any other. She was set down,
Turned round three times,
The blindfold undone.
On her way. On her own.

But docile as Isaac,
He too carried a small bundle of twigs.

The journey was ardourous,
She had labours to perform
Fitting and rightly so
For her station.
Once she had understood
What the word meant,
The role she had to play, heroines
Often have uninteresting parts,

The good can appear dull,
Are seldom permitted the laughs;

All too whitely, O Cordelia
Had an impossible parent,

But obeyed.
She was the one in white,
The one the mountain
Asked for. The lamb
Would not falter her lines.
The cue from the rocks
Would not be missed.

Given the push of birth
We run towards death,
Pushed or pulled
Go that way, willy nilly,

Neither stones nor nodding flowers
Can alter or change direction,
Nor the hours taken blindfold
Or with the eyes open,

We all hold the same token,
A sign on the forehead,
Or on the doorpost under the ivy.

We could have told her
She was set an impossible task.
How many needles in what haystacks
Would she sew shirts of nettles
In the dead of midnight,
Issuing no complaint?

Not all fairy stories
Have happy endings.

The swans rest like china
On the moving waters,
Anchored to their element,
Necks bent.

Daughters are bred
To be obedient.

Smooth down
Smooth down
Dear Mother,

The pure white sheet she said,

Lie down
Lie down
Dear Daughter,

On this your marriage bed.

Listen
My dear
O listen,

Sing roses
White and red.

FIELDS

Banktown.

    Hillfield   Millfield

    Brighton   Bleach,

    Wright's   Scaddons

    Coarse and Rushy,

    Six Acres   Seven Acres

    Troy and Santry

    Top Haggard

    Bottom Haggard.

    Black Shed   Bottoms.

Baltray.

    Garry Hummish   Long Field

    Cowen   High Cowen

    The Haggard

    Cloch Staca.

Auctioneer:

    On two hundred acres of prime farm land . . .

    suitable for fattening and tillage . . . .

God: 'One generation passeth away,
      And another generation cometh:
      but the earth standeth for ever."

Brighton.   The High
                   March hare

                   hums over
                   batterned and bare fields

                   to a rut
                   in the sand.

                   Knife cut
                   of wind

                   a hope
                   in hard air

                   in the lope
                   and pad

                   of jack fox miling
                   to the vixon's keening.

Watch and wait
for the flycatcher and his mate

come late come late
to the alder tree;

loud cackle the cock
and his love hens listen

shell duck and drake
the creaking song

of the corncrake
in the haggard.

Bottoms.   Heavy-headed Bottoms
mayloaded,

drugged by buttercup
primrose celandine

banks and deep ditches
cool and cressed

wild cherry
cheering cheering

dressed overall.

Hawthorn hugged
down down

to the tight sward
thick and right

full of lickings
for lamb and foal

over and over with clover
alive with bees.

Up there
crazy.

Lap the plover
with his lover

twist and flap
flippant and lazy

curl the blue
with fingered pinions;

he makes
space his.

Curlews cruise
and tip the curved

air,
strong-winged

down beat
down beak

steady
steady

to the river
to the shore
to the sea.

Black Shed.   The black shed
is gone now,
fifty years ago
or more, but the name
stands.

A little field
too awkward
to plough, uneven-
shaped, but sheltered
with high hedges
and flaring furze; soon
early bite grows quick,
before milk-easing June.

Here mares
foal down,
and many a heifer
heaved her young to earth.

A good place for birth.

Our first time ever foal
was dropped there,
one night in a sudden wild,
a summer storm.

Small Dermot rushed
the early morning news
                            but we
had felt her coming
in the wind's wet knocking.

Up and over
daylight
lane and field
we went
in the well-washed morning;

homed, by the hedge
the mare, contented, fat
sat back, like a dog
on her haunches.

And this new chocolate life
a clean licked
catkin creature
                    Stood,
Strut up;

High-headed as her dam
(suede nostrils flickering
our hands our faces),
and noticed all this New,

O jade
O jewel,

This morning's miracle.

Cloch Staca.

Guarding the river mouth.   Stones.
Teeth, or eyes watching,
Their unfathomed bulk
Dulled by the centuries; watching.

No enemies come by water,
We do not stand shading our eyes
Peering for a gleaming Viking prow,
They have come. Gone,

And the twin stones stand watching;
They know what Gods were appeased,
What blood what sacrifice
Washed them; and who

Died screaming
At the huge curve of the sky,
The flat of the sea.

Now cattle vegetate, roll their eyes
Pause, lean on those stones to scratch
Their hides, rotating their jaws;
Carved one with the stones; watching

The rising tide;
The continuous moan
Of the sea.

GROWTH

God: The sun riseth, and goeth down,
            and returneth to his place, and there rising again'

ECCLESIASTES 1.5

Auctioneer: This unique property adjacent to all facilities in
                        a sportman's paradise hunting, river and sea-
                        fishing at hand . . . .

 In my rising up and my lying down
Where where is my resting place?
I have left my father's house
And these lands are strange to me.

As I look out over the mud
And the stretches of wild water
I know nothing but my rising up
And lying down; here is order,
Each fulfils and obeys.

Memories of women
Cling to this house,
With them I laugh in the kitchen
Where brown crocks gleam
With white milk.

Down in the dairy
Gold treasures of butter.

Early early in the morning hear
Girls blue and white with
Starched sunlight
Laugh in the lane.
The cows attend them
Singing relief.

Who is our relief Lord?
What is your will for your servants?

Wait for the word
To take place.
I know no action.
Is love something
To learn about with children,
A duty taught, not understood?

Maggie put the chestnuts by the fire;
Who will be her lover?
Who will be her lover?
Who will be yours?

The heat is mounting mounting,
Fat nuts snap explode,
Maggie's heart is beating
Feet run down the road,

Running down the lane boy,
Across the wetted grass
Now beneath the willow
Who can hear her grasp?

Standing by the gate
on a summer evening
when the wind drops,

the rooks swing
into action and reaction
around the chimneys,

carrying the first hint,
the first signal,
that the sap
is no longer rising.

Peace does not come
from anywhere,

but grows
out of the declining day,

and the action
of standing still.

In my rising up and in my lying down
I do the will of the father.

The first decade.

> Restless,
>
> and not
>
> knowing what,
>
> here, under
>
> the ribs
>
> heels life.

> No knowledge,
>
> no will,
>
> the woman
>
> invaded
>
> sits still,
>
> but fingers
>
> flow over beads,

Hail full of grace

> Over the *labhan*
>
> the flash of dunlin dance
>
> light as dreams; days

pattern into nights,
comings and goings
orderings and sowings
good and bad harvests.

Thy will be done,

Deaths and keenings,
up muddy laneways with
baskets, chicken wrapped
in hot linen, taken,
by shaken old fingers.

Blessed art thou

Step back in the shadows
the eyes of the women
quick look to the belly
to notice a coming,

Pray for us sinners

the date and the days
taken into consideration
the months and the years
added and subtracted.
Nothing is missed.

Now and at the hour

.

the village knows it:
its small eyes blinking
like death in the sun.

Blessed is the fruit.

The second decade.

The apple trees usually had a good harvest.
Close to the house, she wandered under the
blossoms,
But, later, found it hard to stretch for fruit,
Some branches, heavy as she, bowed to her.
She could pick and eat.

She would sew there; and feel the feet
Of the child scrabble her stomach.
Laughter would shake fear as rooks
Rise from the trees with a clap of hands.

The third decade.

Waiting is
difficult.
Easier to run
than sit still.

The pile of small linen
grows on the shelves.
Neatly.
Waiting for an end
that is a beginning,
cradle tucked
with warm blankets
perfect and total,
no more
need be added,
no change
is necessary,
round full and tidy
can stay,
as it is.

Ring-a-ring-a-roses
A pocket full of posies

To thee do we cry, poor banished
Children of Eve,
To thee do we send up our sighs
Mourning and weeping
In this vale of tears.

Atishoo, Atishoo,
We all fall down.

The fourth decade.

The river will not stop
this frail bark
my body, will not
answer my calls,

it carries a burden
and I flow
to the unknown sea,
I do not wish

to drown in this,
who
is being born
you or I?

And why
cannot I pull in
this little boat
step off and safely say,

this journey can wait;
I will leave,
until I feel
more adventurous.

Was it love
that pushed
my brown boat out
on the waters?

Was it love
that sent me peering
down into nets
for the salmon of knowledge?

What will I know
when panting and heaving
limbs lead I climb
hair clinging

To the shore?
And those cries
I hear over the water
mingling with sea birds,

are they yours,
or mine?

The fifth decade.

The path she took wound into the hills.

She had no alternative; but along the way

Children joined her. They

Were the point of the journey.

She pressed onwards.

They were her bright summers,

Sleepy autumns,

Bites of winter.

Took up all her time;

Would appear at a bend in the road

To take her hand.

She knew there was no stopping

There was no turning back once

She had set her foot on the path,

Even if she carried a magic branch

As a talisman.

Or three white stones in her pocket.

She had to go through the land of the giants.

Their chatter, cut knees

Scramble after blackberries

Or running ahead with the dog,

Ahead, always ahead,

Kept her mind full, off

Tired feet and aching,

This walking was more than she'd bargained for.

When a boy
Stepped out from the trees
Sending a shower of magpies to heaven
As he snapped a twig,

One for sorrow
Two for joy

She was pleased;
Relieved.

Even if we have been told
By fires in winter, or by
Windows on a summer evening
That good will triumph,
That virtue is rewarded,
There are still those eyes
Gleaming that show no love.
No doors in that darkness.

Three for a girl
Four for a boy,

Things were prepared
A swept house
Candle in the window
The place
Set for a stranger

Then a girl joined her;

Seven arrows,

A full quiver.

Auctioneer: This period house keeps its unique atmosphere
                 because of careful modernisation. Ideal for a
                 family near church and school . . . .

Glory be to the Father
And to the Son
And to the Holy Spirit
As it was in the beginning . . . .

She thought all was provided
managed and ordered
in its place and neatly
that

portions had been found
and daughters married
to men of round substance
with natures not malicious
that

they were good-mannered
tidy and comfortable
without trouble, not bothersome
their Name respectable
that

'rising up in those days
went into the hill country
with haste.'

LUKE 1:39

Sister Sister
never more
Will your winsome
infant leap

Hear the knock
   upon the door
Hear the coming
   of my feet,

Bring O bring no turtledoves.

How you spoke
   with love to me
Of your growing
   family,

You who bore him
   daughters, sons,
Left to die in
   childbirth pangs.

Bring O bring no turtledoves.

   Smooth down
   Smooth down
   Dear Mother

The pale cold sheet she said,

   Kneel down
   Kneel down
   Dear daughter

Close, by your sister's head,

Listen
My dear
O listen,

The song I sang is dead.

Bring O bring no turtledoves.

The child that curls
inside her,

Is carved
And still
As stone.

Pray on
Pray on
Dear daughter

For my heart is lost and gone.

O bring no turtledoves
She sang.
O so sang she:

My babe and I
Are bound to die,

So let the doves fly free.

'A voice in Rama was heard
lamentation and great mourning
Rachel bewailing her children
and would not be comforted,
because they are not.'

MATTHEW 2:18

I am an old woman,
I look O Lord
For guidance;
I who am old.

Now in my winter
I should hold
Death's hand.
She is my rightful sister.

It is me
She should break,
My bare tree withers
In this bony weather.

O foul mistake
To miss this old one,
To make my heart
Shake.

Cruel she is
And hard. Cruel
To take my child
Carrying her child.

I, who am brittle
Of flesh and bone,
Turned to
Stone.

My daughter
Whom I would shelter,
A lamb for slaughter,
Your knife

Cut this lily
White, O my grey head
Who set out
Her wedding bed.

My sorrow
My sorrow,

Bitter the law
Bitter. Made by men,
Who give a daughter
To a man.

Clasped
In his power
Him I would throttle
On him I spit.

Drunk
Hand on the bottle
That throat
His dote his darling!

Not as lovers of old
Bold. His heart
Frog cold.
I shudder.

There was help;
He would not raise a hand,
(Help was near)
Would not,

Answer
A prayer.
Did you Lord
Hear?

You Lord,
You could shake him
Make him.
The husband

Could refuse
Bind or loose
O Death why
Did you not take me?

Cold she is now
And cold the little one.
Not as cold as I,
I long to die.

Lord Lord
I live in deep care
Your thorns press
Through my greying hair;

Blessed Mother
You held a dead son,
How long do I wait
For resurrection?

Give us protection.

God: 'Maketh his rounds by the south
and turneth again to the north:
the spirit goeth forward,
surveying all places around about,
and returneth to his circuits.'

ECCLESIASTES 1.6

Where where

The Hare?

Gone:

Like a stroke
a sickle of light
strike
the day dead.

Where fled?

Where where?

There.

Glitter
the rhythm
of scythe

britter
fell and flow
on our knees

twine
bine
heart and head

throb
noose
thread,

the tightening circle
of sheaves.

Cocoon
curl
She,

Goddess
bread
manna

in what manner
the thread
she weaves

round
      down
through

her labyrinths

before the ebb
and wreck
of wheaten seas.

She runs:

spun
in a circle
of sun,

gilt gold
straw king

topples

chaff royal

burns

the clay red

horizons

overturn,

heads bow

to their knees.

They lie,

sweat and flies

muster,

luster jewels

in the corners

of eyes,

in the blackening

margins

of fields.

        Where

                the Hare

        Where?

        the vacant form,

        is still.

Hand warm.

Who dare?

O dare ye enter
Her circle's centre?

LEAVING

God: 'All the rivers run into the sea;

            yet the sea doth not overflow; into the place

            from whence the rivers come, they return,

            to flow again.'

ECCLESIASTES 1.7

Picture
Obedience:
The prime mover.

The virgin bows her head
accepts the urgent eyeing
of the full-blooded angle,
takes the message to her heart
and head.   Is classically so.
Cool.   Unruffled.   Nobody's fool.
The downcast eyes hide
what is not said.

i

Strange, after years in a land
that was not your own
but taken to the bone.

Each path and dip
and where the trees part
and the shape

of the willow against the sky;
and why small birds return
to the same tree.

A shaft of scent
from the laden shrub
repeats its mood

onto the memory;
with pattern
it repatterns love
for a place.

Bidden to come
Bidden to leave.

This stretching space
this reach of sky,
this edge;

here land tilts over into sea
earth sea river merge
in passion, marriage,

and roaring war,
the mingling of foreign bloods.

Tilth of river
split and seared by salt tongues,
sand, soil, mud, a bond,

familiar war,
a give, a take,
as river pounds

a butting head
into the sea's breath,

rasping stone, easing into sand.
The sea's turbulent converse
with still land.

ii

After her leaving
was there no mark
left to show?

Footprints
in the mud go, fold,
ooze into nothing.

Long skirts brush
through dry leaves,
sweeping a little path.

Soon winds lift
and dart
tracing other
patterns over,

no sign
of the journey.

A light,
bobbing towards,
nearer
blinding,

then away, gone;
no trails on the air
yet,

everything
that touches a thing
changes it.

A love print on
the brain can
scald and bleach.

                                        A squawk of floorboards
                                        A chatter of cups.

        Do trees remember
        who passed under,
        and when

        as they push out
        bud leaf flower
        apple, and again

        allow the sap to seep
        back to the soil,
        standing drained

        for winter,
        heart hardened
        to the stiff breeze?

                                        Hand on the doorknob
                                        Hand on the bannister.

        What is left
        in rooms; a voice
        to echo echo and

fade to nowhere?
Or are they nestling
with spiders

waiting to be spoken again?
Do walls soak in
through every pore

the slash of love,
the gush of birth,
the act of death?

iii

Leaving is death:
Big or little
a dying.

The place you live in
takes you, slowly,
like a good lover,
easing you into itself.

Opening secrets
gradually,
the muse seeping
like blood.

Leaving
is a minor
crucifixion,

little murder
small death.

Night takes over
and devours, so

the next step
the next day

can open
a possible mouth.

Auctioneer: Although this property has been vacant
                                      for some time, it is in sound condition.
                                      And the old-world charm of the house
                                      and garden offer exciting opportunities
                                      to a person of taste . . . .

                                      Now is a moveable feast.

Song: The birds of the trees
              Have a place to sing
          The cows in the fields
              Have a hollow;
          The fish in the sea
              Swim wide and free
          But I come and go as the swallow.

          I was told to come
              Now told to go
          My husband's wrath
              I must swallow
          My love that has grown
              Must not be shown
          For I obey and follow.

          I must take my children
              I must take my bed
          Only Christ can share
              My sorrow;
          The song I sing is
              Obedience,
          Wrapped around with
              Fear of tomorrow.

          The birds in the trees
              Have a place to rest
          The rabbit has his burrow.

No place

In this world

   Belongs to me,

So I must beg and borrow.

WINTER. THE WOMAN

God: What is it that hath been?

The same thing that shall be?

What is it that hath been done?

The same that shall be done.

ECCLESIASTES 1.9

What pain ails me

What fear nails me

The moon full gliding?

No winds wild blowing

No rains soft knowing

Takes this dread dying.

The bracken makes a bed

For winter's maiden head

For this cold crying.

Why do I feel
  The moon is a sister
Her pallid face
  Is my reflection?

Where are the feet
  Who ran stairs quickly,
I would have the sun
  For a brother.

Why does this pale woman
  Pause at my window
Her twisted face
  Reminds me of pain?

Red roses accuse
  My white fingers fumble,
How can there be
  Bad blood between us?

I sit here
  In a windless corner,
Feeling the cold
  As if blood were rain.

Little Lord of death
　　Take a mighty step
Dance, Dance,
　　To the High Hop tune;
Dance, Dance,
　　With the lady fair
Who plays her flute
　　To the jealous moon.

Little Lord of death
　　Your feet come soon
They know each step
　　In the jig and rune,
They know each step
　　As the lady fair
Shows a clean heel
　　In the grass in June.

As the young girls played
　　On a summer's day,
As the young girls tinkled
　　A piano tune;
And sang sentimental
　　And played violins
Never knowing you were bowing
　　Your Nick Nock tune.

In a house by the sea
    That they took for the summer
If help came late,
    If help came soon;
Little Lord of death
    Had ticked off a number
A tired little number,
    In a rented room.

    Dance, Dance,
Mighty Lord of Death
    Dance High
To your hip hop tune,
    The rose that was red
Is the rose that is white
    And she fell down dead
In a rented room.

    The roses white
And the roses red
    They burst with joy
When they're in bloom,
    They sink and sigh
And sodden lie,
    When they open their ears
To your Nick Nock tune.

God: 'All things are hard: man cannot explain them by word.

The eye is not filled with seeing, neither is the ear filled

with hearing.'

ECCLESIASTES 1.8

Words were shut in his head.

He was not trained in the art of touching,

To fondle bodies or words;

Was only easy with horses.

The talk of men he understood.

Lines dictated by time, weather and harvest.

Neighbours who trusted his tongue,

Would come to him to settle arguments

Of rights and boundaries.

Was known to be better than the law.

And cost nothing.

Books, their broad backs contented.

He could handle their silences.

But women. How they flitted

And felt and did, how they gave in.

Knotted the world up carefully always

Putting away in drawers and doing.

His mouth stayed shut.

When thoughts tickled and scuttled his brain,
He had no broad paths, no passageways,
No escape. Then inbred, they circled
And coupled, slim animals, these green ideas,
Slow-growing monsters, shoving, snouting,
At his firm bars.

How he held them.
Gripped his mind calloused as hand
Schooled to the pull of leather;
Until sweat ran off the back of his soul.
They turned worlds over,
Jumbled and jostled for notice.
He gave none.

But when the red shook him he was done.

Then, as if apart from him a mad dam burst
A vast roar, wave on volcanic wave, his voice
Spilled, drowning in the spume
Of his dead song.

He has lost his white Queen,
He stands alone
at the mercy of pawns.

The swift Queen weakened,
now is gone.
Those last steps.

into the wings,
her final exit.

He always hoped
her part was written
into the third act;

that suddenly
she would come
through the curtain

all forgiven.

Now his eyes dagger
the pages, fingers
fever out lines

but her name
is nowhere
in the script.

How could such
a happening
happen to him?

So many props
to remind him,

rummaging in a drawer
uncovers an old
purse or button;

on a flyleaf
in a book
her name appears;

repeating his
familiar prayers
he catches her look,

he always counted
on playing that
scene again;

getting the lines
perfect at last,
make it go with a swing.

Now on the bare
stage
he plays the part

of the dying King,
(no, not anyway original)
must keep this old

show going.
Keep up the pace
or make a new start,

but a King
can move only
one square at a time,

though he knows
the supporting cast
are trying to help

will prompt
if he misses a line

even if they are
afraid of his
fiery temperament.

Neither tears
nor rage
console him;

nor neighbours
who come in the evenings
sharing a glass,

talking, until
their chairs
scrape back the dawn.

He knows
his performance
is slipping,

that he mumbles
his part.

Knows
the producer's eyes
are on him,

slowly,
lowering
the Mask.

Auctioneer: This gentleman's residence is very secluded;

          would suit executive, with expansive views,

          is near all amenities of town and country,

          river and sea . . . .

Are you coming by night

 by water
 by holocaust
 by motor car or
 by accident?

Are you coming?

 Dressed in royal garments
 anointed with chrism
 with blessings
 by fire
 with brimstone
 with hair lacquer.

Are you coming?

 Often or now
 or not now or never
 or tomorrow or

the Wednesday after
next?

The old bull lay dying
but they

kept their distance
for fear of a last twist of that
mighty head.

The rest
fled,

scurrying and disorderly
bickering for inheritance.

The old bull
lay in the dust.

They kept watch,
waiting,
for the timekeeper.

This space from morning to evening
is longer than ever
than this ever
or ever after.

The children,
two daughters
one son,

crept closer,

brought water,
for the old bull lay
dying.

They had their duty
and knew there
were things that must

things they had to face
and the space between now
and then must be filled

carefully
with ritual.

The candles lighted.

Because they could now
see clearer than ever before,

each flame

a new opening

in the dark.

Giving a place

to the space in the head.

The old bull lay dying.

His black shoulders

his pulse marking

tickering tickering,

The bull alone on a circle of sand.

Red from his nostrils

gold of his horns

move as a blessing.

What is he minding

in that deep cranium,

wounds in the mind

that have inward bled?

The days of dominion

when a stamp of his hooves

a lowering head

brought the tribe to its knees:

now the tongue lodged
and lead.

Clasping of fingers
dropping of eyes
why are we kneeling?

'He is one of the old ones'
the Timekeeper said.

'Belonging to times that
are not now.'

His thumb pressed
the stop-watch

Dead.

The black bull lay still

the clan scattered
and fled.

God: 'Nothing under the sun is new, neither is any man able to say: Behold this is new. For it hath already gone in the ages that were before us.'

ECCLESIASTES 1:10

I planned a salvation
It lead to a death;
Your death is my death,
But I planned a salvation.

Making and remaking
The buying of land
The song of the kettle
The litter of kittens

Trips to the town
And shoes for the children
The looped-up curtains
Covered emotions

Chairs draped with cretonnes
Dusting and duties
Tossing and turning
With typhus fever

The cry in the night
God's will be done.

The talk in the village
Chatter in the drawingroom
The door partly opened,
Then shut.

Now is moveable.

I prayed a salvation
My prayer was answered
With death by water,
But I prayed a salvation.

Leaves twitter and blind
Into corners,
Caught in clumps
To lose their crisp
Under drips from downpipes

Before things fall apart
Worms gobble, moth dart
And pulpy maggots move in
To chew, hawk, and spit
On the heart

Auctioneer: We have no hesitation
                In strongly advising
                an early viewing
                of this unique property . . . .

                As it was in the beginning
                is now . . . .